American Alligator

by Ellen Lawrence

Consultant:

Bryan P. Piazza, PhD
Director, Freshwater and Marine Science
The Nature Conservancy, Louisiana Chapter
Baton Rouge, Louisiana

New York, New York

Credits

Cover, © Arto Hakola/Shutterstock; 4, © Steve Oehlenschlager/Shutterstock; 5, © David Osborn/Shutterstock; 6, © Cosmographics; 7, © Tim Graham/Alamy; 8T, © tome123/Shutterstock; 8B, © Eric Isselee/Shutterstock; 9, © mangojuicy/Shutterstock; 10T, © Brberrys/Shutterstock; 10B, © tome123/Shutterstock; 11, © Nancy Nehring/iStock; 12T, © UrosPoteko/iStock; 12B, © Steve Byland/Shutterstock; 13, © Martin Woike, NiS/Minden Pictures/FLPA; 14, © Rudy Umans/Shutterstock; 15, © Tom Salyer/Alamy; 16, © Michael Patrick O'Neill/Alamy; 17, © Kerstin Layer/Alamy; 18, © NASA Photo/Alamy; 19, © Wayne Lynch/All Canada Photos/Alamy; 20T, © David Kjaer/Nature Picture Library; 20B, © Brian Lasenby/Shutterstock; 21, © Orhan Cam/Shutterstock; 22L, © Diana Taliun/Shutterstock; 22R, © Hurst Photo/Shutterstock; 23TL, © Nancy Nehring/IstockPhoto; 23TC, © &#169 Robert/iStock; 23TR, © Dariush M/Shutterstock; 23BL, © Evoks24/Shutterstock; 23BC, © Willie Davis/Shutterstock; 23BR, © Ulysses ua/Shutterstock.

Publisher: Kenn Goin
Senior Editor: Joyce Tavolacci
Creative Director: Spencer Brinker
Design: Emma Randall
Photo Researcher: Ruby Tuesday Books Ltd

Library of Congress Cataloging-in-Publication Data

Names: Lawrence, Ellen, 1967– author.
Title: American alligator / by Ellen Lawrence.
Description: New York, New York : Bearport Publishing, [2017] | Series: Swamp
  things: animal life in a wetland | Audience: Ages 7–11. | Includes
  bibliographical references and index.
Identifiers: LCCN 2016012091 (print) | LCCN 2016015638 (ebook) | ISBN
  9781944102517 (library binding) | ISBN 9781944997175 (ebook)
Subjects: LCSH: American alligator—Juvenile literature. | CYAC: Alligators.
Classification: LCC QL666.C925 L39 2017 (print) | LCC QL666.C925 (ebook) |
  DDC 597.98/4—dc23
LC record available at https://lccn.loc.gov/2016012091

For more information, write to Bearport Publishing Company, Inc., 45 West 21st Street, Suite 3B, New York, New York 10010. Printed in the United States of America.

10 9 8 7 6 5 4 3 2 1

Contents

Mealtime!

It's evening in the Atchafalaya (*uh*-chaf-uh-LYE-uh) **Swamp**, and a duck is paddling in a shallow lake.

Suddenly, an American alligator shoots out of the water.

It snaps at the bird with its huge jaws.

The terrified duck flaps its wings and escapes.

Slowly, the alligator sinks back beneath the water to wait for its next meal.

wood duck

An alligator is a type of **reptile**. This group of animals includes crocodiles, turtles, lizards, and snakes.

American alligator

5

An Alligator's World

American alligators live in warm areas in the southern United States.

They make their homes in rivers, lakes, and swampy areas like the Atchafalaya.

In a swamp, most of the land is covered by water.

Alligators spend a lot of time in the water, but they also live on damp, muddy land.

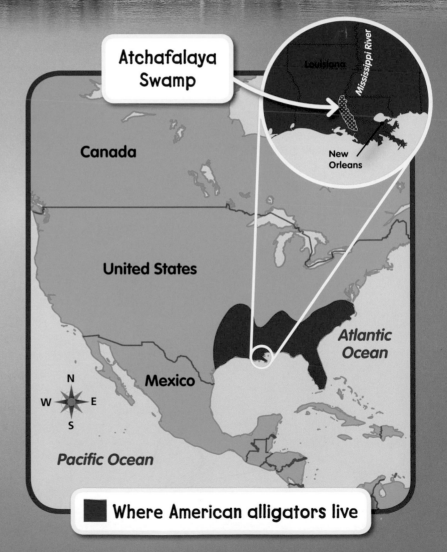

Atchafalaya Swamp

Louisiana

Mississippi River

Canada

New Orleans

United States

Atlantic Ocean

Mexico

Pacific Ocean

N W E S

■ Where American alligators live

The American alligator is the largest reptile in the United States.

How would you describe an American alligator to someone who has never seen one?

Meet an American Alligator

An American alligator has a large body with short legs, a wide **snout**, and a long tail.

Its body is covered with hard bony plates called **scutes**.

An alligator has up to 80 teeth that can easily crunch through bones.

When its teeth wear down or fall out, it grows new teeth.

During its lifetime, an alligator may go through 3,000 teeth!

scutes

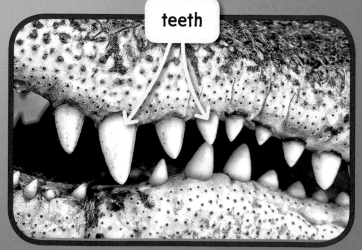

teeth

nostrils

An adult male alligator can grow up to 15 feet (4.6 m) long and can weigh 1,000 pounds (454 kg). Female alligators are smaller. They can grow to about 8 feet (2.4 m) long and weigh about 200 pounds (91 kg).

An alligator's nostrils are located on top of its snout. How do you think this helps the animal in its watery home?

Swamp Life

Often, an alligator floats just below the surface of the water.

Only the animal's eyes and its nostrils stay above the water.

This allows the reptile to see and to breathe.

To swim, an alligator swishes its long, powerful tail from side to side.

nostrils

an alligator swimming

Like all reptiles, alligators are cold-blooded, which means their bodies aren't naturally warm. To warm up, alligators sit on land and soak up the sun's heat.

On the Hunt

Alligators hunt both in the water and on land.

Adult alligators eat fish, crabs, frogs, turtles, and water birds.

They also hunt and eat larger animals, such as nutrias, raccoons, and even deer.

When an alligator grabs a small animal, it usually swallows it whole!

a type of water bird called a heron

nutria

Sometimes, an alligator catches an animal that's too big to be swallowed whole. Then the alligator twists and shakes its **prey** until a piece that's small enough to be swallowed falls off.

an alligator eating a turtle

13

Gator Holes

When it's very hot, alligators create shallow pools called gator holes.

To make a gator hole, an alligator wriggles its body back and forth in the mud.

These powerful movements make a large hole in the ground.

Soon, rainwater and water from nearby streams and ponds fill the hole.

The alligator then settles into the pool to relax and cool off.

an alligator wriggling in mud

In very hot weather, some ponds and streams in a swamp dry up. Sometimes, extra-deep gator holes stay filled with water. The holes provide a home for fish, turtles, and other swamp animals.

a gator in its hole

15

Huge Nests

In spring, male and female alligators come together to **mate**.

After mating, a female finds a spot near the water.

She builds a large nest using sticks, leaves, and mud and lays up to 50 eggs in it.

Then she covers the eggs with more leaves and mud to keep them warm.

After about 60 days, the baby alligators are ready to hatch!

a female alligator guarding her nest

A female alligator stays close to her eggs. She guards them from raccoons and other animals that want to eat them.

16

Squeaking Babies

Once the baby alligators hatch, they make squeaking noises.

This lets the mother alligator know to remove the mud and leaves covering the nest.

Then the babies climb out of the nest and into the nearby water.

Sometimes a mother alligator carries the babies to the water in her mouth.

Soon, the babies start hunting for small animals, such as fish and snails.

a baby alligator hatching from an egg

Growing Up in the Swamp

The baby alligators stay close to their mother for about one year.

Then each young alligator finds its own place to live in the swamp.

An alligator can grow as much as 10 inches (25 cm) each year.

After about 10 years, it is an adult.

However, it keeps growing for its entire life!

baby alligator

mother alligator

young alligator

An alligator can live to be 50 years old.

Science Lab

Draw a Life-Size American Alligator

An adult male alligator can grow to be 15 feet (4.6 m) long from its snout to the end of its tail. The tail is about 7.5 feet (2.3 m) long.

On a playground or sidewalk, use chalk and a measuring tape to make a life-size drawing of an alligator.

Add these labels to your drawing:

tail	scutes	leg	body	nostrils	snout

Science Words

mate (MAYT) to come together to produce young

prey (PRAY) an animal that is hunted and eaten by another animal

reptile (REP-tile) a cold-blooded animal, such as a lizard or turtle, that has dry, scaly skin, a backbone, and lungs

scutes (SKYOOTS) hard, bony plates, or sections, on an alligator's skin

snout (SNOUT) the long front part of an animal's face that includes its nose and mouth

swamp (SWAHMP) a wetland habitat where trees and bushes grow from the water-covered land

23

Index

Read More

Jackson, Tom. *Saltwater Crocodile (The Deep End: Animal Life Underwater).* New York: Bearport (2014).

Potts, Steve. *American Alligators (North American Animals).* Mankato, MN: Capstone (2012).

Royston, Angela. *Alligator: Killer King of the Swamp (Top of the Food Chain).* New York: Rosen (2014).

Learn More Online

To learn more about American alligators, visit **www.bearportpublishing.com/SwampThings**

About the Author

Ellen Lawrence lives in the United Kingdom. Her favorite books to write are those about nature and animals. In fact, the first book Ellen bought for herself when she was six years old was the story of a gorilla named Patty Cake that was born in New York's Central Park Zoo.